To:
Ms. Robinson.
Thank you for your p
to Gabrielle Burton's success.

MyAnn Rath
2018-2019

There's Healing after Hurt

By Katrina Hurst

With MyChana Burton

© 2018 by Katrina Hurst / Way Agile
All rights reserved. This book or any portion thereof may not be reproduced or used in any manner whatsoever without the express written permission of the publisher except for the use of brief quotations in a book review.

First Printing, September 2018

ISBN 978-1-7325672-0-7 (eBook)

WAY Agile Publishing
P. O. Box 165704
Irving, TX 75016
www.wayagile.com
www.HealingAfterHurt.org

Letter, Editing, Prologue, Epilogue and Journal Elements

By MyChana Burton

Front and Rear Cover Design by Darren Thomas

Book Design by WAY Agile

Contents

Letter from the Editor: *6*
Prologue *8*
Who Am I? *11*
The Night I Found Out *14*
The Unexpected Detour *18*
The Day *21*
Take time to grieve *24*
Have a support system *28*
Be accountable to someone *31*
Don't Blame Yourself *34*
Press Through *37*
Make that Baby Proud *40*
Remember where they are! *43*
You're Still a Mother! *46*
Be Determined *49*
Remember God's Promises *52*
Renew Your Mind *55*
Speak Life into Yourself *58*
Speak things into Existence *61*
Have Faith *64*
Rediscover You *67*
Don't let the devil steal your joy! *70*
Don't hide behind your family *73*
Only the Strong Survive? *76*

Remember what you wanted	79
The Transition	82
Love Yourself	85
Prune Unproductivity	88
Expect Greatness	91
Take Care of You	94
Comfort Someone Else	97
Don't Let Pity Control You	100
Be True to Yourself	103
Be Hopeful*	106
Go Forward	109
Be Transparent	111
Thank God for Restoration	114
They don't understand, but they understand	117
Don't Give up on God	120
Pray to God	123
God knew who to Trust	126
Feed Me (Studying the Bible)	128
All this from that	131
Epilogue	134
Letter to Jayla Kindell Carter	138
Share Your Story Or A Letter To Your Lost Love One.	141
The Call to Action – Share Your Story	141
The Call to Action – Write a letter to you lost little love.	145
Discussion Group Questions	147

Letter from the Editor:

I am excited to invite you to take this journey to a new you. Whether you are reading the story of Katrina's journey for the first, fifth or tenth time, if you are anything like me you will find nuggets of wisdom each time.

In this 1st Edition in print there is a new element to help you to begin your journey; it goes a step further and takes your understanding a bit deeper. Each section is followed by question and/or writing prompts that challenge you to dig deep within yourself to find a greater understanding of yourself that leads to living your best you. Utilize the space provided to write notes, journal and/or write additional questions you would like to explore.

Your first time through, you may not find every section applicable, but I challenge you to revisit those sections as you become more self-aware, your confidence grows, and your boldness expands. I believe at some point or another you will be blessed by each section and the enlightenment they bring.

"There's Healing after Hurt" is more than about the loss of a child, as it is also about loss in general and the pain that unexpected/ unprepared for change can bring. I challenge you to use a love for God, and a love for yourself as the best way to learn to love and be love properly.

From my first time through reading Katrina's story to my twenty plus times as I prayed through the process of asking relevant and thought-provoking questions and writing prompts for you to use this book as a journal and/or workbook of sorts, to grow spiritually, emotionally and relationally.

God's Grace and Peace be with you always,

MyChana Burton, MBA, SA, PST, CSM

CEO -WAY Agile

Prologue

All of her life the one thing she wanted more than anything in this world is to be a mommy. From her childhood with six younger siblings, she had plenty of opportunities to play mommy, in her own bossy way. Sure, she knows the nursery rhyme, "first comes love, then comes marriage, then comes Katrina with the baby carriage. "That is the ideal sequence, but it wasn't the case for Katrina. She was a young college student nearing the end of completing her associate degree. Then, the test was positive, and the abundance of joy was real.

Plans, preparations, hopes and dreams for the baby she carried were always evolving in her mind. Then in a moment it all changes, premature birth, one hour of life and tears that would not stop falling. Emotions all over the place denial (this is just a bad dream), anger (why me), bargaining (I just wanted one baby), depression (I can't live without her), and acceptance (I don't understand, but everything happens for a reason). These very real emotions are the Kubler-Ross Grief Cycle, also known as the 5 Stages of Grief.

The 5 stages of grief are more of a cycle with progressions and regressions, which is normal and to be expected. No two people handle loss the same and therefore, no two people experience loss the same, the only thing we know is that one or all five stages will happen as a result of a loss. There are no expectations, which can realistically be placed on how long, when and/or to which extent the griever will experience any stage, at any given time. The two stages grievers tend to easily repeat and/or get stuck are depression and anger, and those are often the longest stages. The stages give the grievers' emotions an identity and allow those that may be experiencing grief and those around them, to validate their feelings, as normal.

In "There's Healing after Hurt" Katrina experiences each stage at some point and some multiple times. *Are the stages clearly identifiable?*

Who Am I?
"God created man in His own image, in the image of God He created him; male and female He created them."
Genesis 1:27 NASB

My name is Katrina Hurst. I am from Detroit, Michigan (Go Blue), and I am the second oldest of 8 children. I am a twin, but I came 12 minutes later than my sister Latina did, and she lets everyone know it too.

My mother, Krystal who was 15 when she had my sister and me, was a single mother most of my childhood and raised all 8 of us. As we were growing up, so was my mother. Our life was not always sunshine, but my mother did the best she could, based on the knowledge and maturity that she had. Therefore, I understood and took the responsibility of being "wise beyond my years," so to speak.

My sister and I had to take care of our siblings while my mother worked. We cleaned (because my mom was not having a nasty house), cooked, and baby sat our younger siblings. I thought I was grown when I started to whoop my little sisters and brothers for their misbehaviors. We also had to make sure we were all ready and went to school. Sometimes it was tough, but I thank God for it because it made me a more responsible teenager and adult. This also fueled my passion for working with children. When we would play games, we loved to play "school". Can anyone guess who the teacher was, always? You guessed it, yours truly.

As a child, I always had a certain drive and determination. I was convinced that I would be something great. Growing up where we did and seeing the struggle that some people had to go through because of their own decisions, I always told myself that "I AM NOT

GOING TO BE A STATISTIC". I was not going to be someone's "sometimes woman", or "a gold digger". Am I perfect? Absolutely not, but I was able to thrive in areas of my life that truly mattered.

I was able to pass each of my elementary classes with honor roll. I was able to pass middle school and receive multiple honor roll accomplishments and play basketball a year before I was supposed to. I was able to graduate high school and be inducted into the National Honor Society. In addition to this I obtained my Associates Degree in Early Childhood Education from Columbus State Community College. I also plan on going back to school to earn my Bachelors in ECE. My last year of college is when I lost my daughter and I was able (by the grace and mercy of God) through all of my tears, heart ache, doubt, and feelings of unworthiness, stick it out and persevere to graduate.

Am I saying all of this to toot my own horn? No, I pray that this will help someone know that no matter what "You ARE going to make it", and to never give up on your dreams. Now that you know a little about my life, here is when my life was forever changed.

Who are you? It is not an uncommon occurrence for someone you meet to ask you "So, tell me a little bit about you?" What is your typical response? Thinking about it now how would you describe yourself? Your childhood? Your upbringing?

The Night I Found Out

It was about 8pm on a Saturday. I was telling my then boyfriend that I hadn't been feeling well. I didn't know why I was feeling like this because I was eating healthy and going to the gym regularly. The obvious sign of pregnancy (lack of a menstrual) was not a concern because I've always been irregular. So, I was talking to him about how I had been feeling and he said, "you might be pregnant" and started laughing. I told him that I thought about that and it may be a possibility. So, I told him that we needed to go to Kroger's and get a test. So, that night we both went and got a pregnancy test. When we got back I took the test immediately. Within minutes the stick said positive. I instantly got excited and started imagining all these amazing things we would do as a family.

Now in the previous section, I told you that I have a big family, and we talk about everything, so my next instinct was to call me mom and sisters. However, it just so happened that my boyfriend's mom was in town spending the week with us, he snatched my phone and told me that we were going to tell his mom first. So, we went upstairs together and told her. She was so excited that she got us more excited. Then said we had to celebrate, so she went to the store and got some champagne and told me I had to drink water.

After that I called my mom and she was equally excited, so much so she would not let me off the phone. When I finally got off the phone with her, my boyfriend and I took our first picture as a pregnant couple.

That Monday, my boyfriend and I, my little sister and his good friend that was staying with us for the summer went down to Planned

Parenthood to get an official pregnancy test and ultrasound. The doctor checked me, she said everything looked good, I was four weeks along, and she gave me my very first ultrasound photo. I was so happy because I was ready to be a mommy. Before I found out that I was pregnant I was not having any sickness, just feeling weird, but after I found out it was like the flood gates opened and I was sick every morning. I did not have weird cravings. I just wanted ice cream, pizza, and chocolate, every day. I think that's about all I really ate all 5 months.

With all the excitement going around, there was one person that I was afraid to tell. My Godmother Denise, who was and still is a very important part of my Christian walk and some of the values that I still hold on to today. There was a portion of my life that I lived with her and she taught me things, I never knew about God and how to be a woman. Even though I was grown and living on my own, it was still hard for me to tell her, because I didn't do it, in the proper order (marriage then baby).

So, I drove to her house, the whole time trying to find the right words to tell her. I was so nervous. So, I got there, and we sit down and then I said, "I have something to tell you". She asked what was wrong and I blurt out "I'm pregnant". She just sat there quietly and smiled a little. At this point I didn't know what to do then finally she said, "I already knew, I was just waiting for you to tell me". I was baffled; she hugged me and said congratulations. She did say, "This isn't the way that it was supposed to be done, but this baby is a blessing". As I left her house, I let out a sigh of relief and thanked God that she didn't judge me or make me feel bad.

In relation to my walk with God, at that time, I was not going to church. Although I still felt convicted because, I wasn't in church and I was not married, I asked God for forgiveness. At this point, that was all I could do. There was one Sunday, I went to church with my Godmother and she said she sensed something going on with the baby and prayed for my baby and me. I believe that God used her to give me strength about what was about to transpire, in a few weeks from then, that neither of us knew.

Who has been the person, you have had the hardest time confessing things about yourself to? Are there things that you were excited about when they happened, but still had one or two people that you knew would not or may not react with the same level of excitement?

The Unexpected Detour

During my last doctor's appointment, I was able to hear her strong heartbeat and I found out that she was indeed a girl. On the way to that appointment we were talking about names. At the time all my siblings had given their children names' starting with the letter J and that was going to be the first letter of my baby's name, as well. So, I came up with her first name Jayla. I'm not sure where we came up with her middle name Kindell, but her last name Carter came from her father.

At the time that I got pregnant I was in school getting my Associates in Early Childhood Development. While I was in school, I had symptoms but nothing that would prevent me from going to school. I was doing well in school and I prided myself in being able to maintain a high GPA, even while being pregnant.

The day before that heartbreaking event, it was a holiday. We had a party at our house. All the family was set to come over and we were going to BBQ. When all the family got there, we cooked and had fun together as a family. At one point in the day, my sister and I even argued about the amount of food. That day I wasn't really worried about my pregnancy, I was a little stressed out about the party because of normal family things, but nothing too much. As family cookouts usually go, we were up late playing cards and games. Never in a million years did I think, everything would change the next day. When Jayla was born she was 14 ounces and 10 inches. The doctor said it may have happened because I have a negative blood type and my blood, and her bloods were fighting against each other. The doctor said usually, I would have been given a shot, before I got pregnant and then another after I gave birth and I would have been fine. I believe that this may have been the reason that she passed although there was no autopsy.

Now that you know a little about me and my life, this is when I thought my life was over!

What life changing event blindsided you? Was it your child you looked forward to, was born to soon and/or was never able to live its full life?

The Day

"The LORD is near to the brokenhearted and saves those who are crushed in spirit."
Psalms 34:18 NASB

The time was about 7:30 am on May 27th, 2008. I was 5 months pregnant, lying in bed and I started to feel a heavy pain (I now know those pains were contractions). I thought it was normal labor pains because I had never been pregnant before to compare the pain to, so I tried to take some medication. The moment I took it I then had to vomit. So, I got up and went into the bathroom. After the medication came back up I felt a rush of release and looked down to see my inner thigh and legs with blood and wetness running down. I said to myself "Lord it's not time". "She's not big enough". So, I called my boyfriend at the time and the father of my child called 911.

On the way to the hospital I silently prayed to God that my baby would be ok. I pleaded with God and asked Him to spare her life and let me be a mom. So, I get to the hospital and they hook me up to all kinds of machines. I told the nurse to turn the monitors away because I didn't want to see my baby fading away. I tried to keep a positive mind and think "God can do anything". The doctor walked into the room, puts his hand on my knee and said, "She's not going to make it". Before any procedure, any interventions they could have tried after she was born, he was counting her out, when he said that I was crushed. Something inside of me let go of all hope. As tears rolled down my face I began to imagine life without her. All my dreams and aspirations I had for her went straight out of the window. I was lost. The doctor comes back and said "ok you are losing too much blood, we have to do a C-section right now. They medicated me and stuck a needle in my back. During the procedure while I'm in and out consciousness, they do what I had been dreading all morning. They take my premature baby from my wound. And just like that all the plans I had went with her. While under anesthesia, I hear her cry and they give her to her father. He shows me how she looks but I can't really focus. The doctors take her away. Jayla Kindell Carter passed away 60 minutes later. To me, life as I knew it was over.

What day in your life would you say was "that day", the day that life as you knew it changed forever? Sometimes things don't always feel like sunshine and sometimes it gets dark. Who are the people that support and encourage you?

Take time to grieve

""Blessed are those who mourn, for they shall be comforted." Matthew 5:4 NASB

After that day, I didn't know what to do. When I was in the hospital recovering all the nurses were so nice. They gave me anything I wanted. My family and friends came to visit. But, still going with the flow, I was so empty. At night when everyone went home, and everything was quiet I would just cry. But even that wouldn't help. The nurses and social workers came in and gave me pamphlets for therapy and grief counseling, but I told them I would be ok. I didn't really express to them how I was really feeling. After being at the hospital for 5 days it was time to go home. When I got home I laid in the very spot that the pain started to happen. A rush of emotions came back to me. And like I always do, I hid them in the back of my mind because I really didn't want to deal with it. I have a very large family and they all periodically came over. My grandparents and my aunt came down from Detroit just to check on me. I laughed and talked with my family. I told everyone I was ok (I wasn't). I said, "God has a reason", but inside I felt hollow and empty. I just kept wondering what the reason was.

One day I was home alone, and I went into her room and looked at all the things her dad and I had bought her and all the things that were given and bought for her. I looked at her crib and the first t-shirt her father had brought her. I remember teasing him when he bought it home because it was a preemie onesie instead of a 0 to 3-month onesie. As I looked around I began to cry uncontrollably. I thought "this isn't fair God", "I only wanted one", "what did I do to deserve this", "I'm very knowledgably and equipped to raise a child". I was falling into a state of depression. But, when anyone was around I put on a "brave face". I couldn't let them see me cry. I was, after all, the "strong one" in the family, the one who "always has it together". I wouldn't let anyone see my hurt; therefore, no one could help me heal from my hurt. Therefore, I never really grieved.

It wasn't until I went to a "regular" (it wasn't nowhere near regular), bible class service at my church Rebirth Worship Center that God really helped me to grieve. I went to church thinking it was going to be a normal service. Boy did God have different plans for that night. It turned out to be a prayer service. Now this service happened years after my daughter passed. All this time I had been holding it in. Can you imagine the damage I was doing to myself and my mind? As we were praying, Pastor Darren Thomas came over to me and started hugging me. I broke down. He started praying for my healing, for my strength, for depression and low self-esteem to leave, and a host of other problems. At this point he knew I lost my daughter, but I never told him how I was feeling. But when God and the Holy Spirit is at work, there is no need for me to open my mouth. I just cried and cried. This time it wasn't my normal "blame game", "I'm so depressed", cry. It was different. As tears flowed I felt depression leave and chains began to fall. I felt my hope and joy come back. I felt my newness coming and beginning to feel whole again. Then after Pastor Darren finished praying for me another member at my church embraced me and started praying. Then she asked me what my pain was. I told her that my daughter had died years earlier and she said that I hadn't had time to grieve. She was right! I had just pushed my feelings and my life went back to life as normal. But thank God, she had the spirit of discernment. She pulled me closer and I begin to cry louder and louder. I felt all my baggage that I had been carrying start falling. That was something I haven't felt in a long time.

We have to let go and let the ALL MIGHTY GOD heal our pains and wounds. It's ok to be vulnerable and give your cares to God. It is also ok to seek, (I'm going to say the forbidden word), therapy. Don't hold things in because it will only cause more pain and hurt. You will be ready to give up and hide in a corner as I did if you do. Dealing with the pain has to be part of your healing process. We need to truly intend on being happy again. You will still have the hurt but eventually you will smile again. I encourage you to find someone who you can confide in. Find someone whether it is a best friend, Pastor, or counselor, to talk and open up about your pain and the things that are going on will take some of the discomfort away.

What people or things have you not grieved? How can you acknowledge and start the grieving process?

Have a support system.

"from whom the whole body, being fitted and held together by what every joint supplies, according to the proper working of each individual part, causes the growth of the body for the building up of itself in love." Ephesians 4:16 NASB

Me being the woman I am and not wanting to "burden" my family with my problems, I just didn't talk about it. It was life as usual. At this point I had given all her things away to people who needed it for their children. I didn't cry in front of people or even talk about my feelings. My family would ask "how am I doing?" and I would say "oh I'm good". What I should have been saying is "I'm broken", "I don't know what to do", "if you could see inside of me", "can you please pray with me". A support system can break you out of your toughest situations. It can heal you with just a touch or a conversation. Do not be afraid to go to a person you can trust and cry on their shoulder and tell them how you are feeling. That person or those people can be the very line between depression and healing. Do not try to do it alone. If God wanted us to handle things alone I don't think he would have created Eve for Adam. Alone is a dark place. I had so many people around me that I could have called on, but I kept it bottled in. Then I found myself getting mad for no reason or snapping at people for minor things they did. This was totally out of character for me because I was usually a happy person. To this day, I'm always smiling. But at that point I let my unwillingness to use my support system, bring me to a place where I literally didn't recognize myself. You say, you don't have anyone? Guess what, you definitely do. God is always going to be the very best support system that you can ever have. Lean on him and tell him all your problems, worries, things that are hard for you to deal with and He will comfort you. He did it for me and He will do it for you as well.

Sometimes things are not always sunshine, and we get low emotionally; in these times we need people in our lives that can uplift and encourage us. Who is supportive and encourages you?

Be accountable to someone

"Bear one another's burdens, and thereby fulfill the law of Christ."
Galatians 6:2 NASB

In my pursuit to healing, I had to eventually be accountable to someone. I had to start sharing my pains and how I felt. That was the only way I would get through it and keep the hope that I felt after God delivered me. Don't get me wrong, there were times that I thought the bottom was going to fall from under me. I started talking to my former Pastor before I start going to Rebirth about my feelings. I had to tell him how I was feeling. I had to share my worries. I had to stop draining my mind into useless television and numbing the pain with drinking and going out (I always felt uncomfortable being there anyway). So, I started writing my feelings down. Also, I started writing letters to Jayla. When I did that, it was the best healing that I could have ever gotten. I started finding solace in my nieces and nephews (and I have a lot of them). I started doing more with them and showing the love and support that only an aunt can show. I started to believe what I wrote to Jayla and it blessed my soul. And in those moments, I was accountable to someone other than my bad feelings and low regard for myself. So, I urge you to find someone to be accountable to.

Who are your accountability partners? Who challenges you to not stay stuck? *There is a reason why, it is a known fact, that having a workout partner makes sticking to your workout goals is accountability. Who are the people that partner with you to hold you accountable for your actions?*

Don't Blame Yourself

"And the great dragon was thrown down, the serpent of old who is called the devil and Satan, who deceives the whole world; he was thrown down to the earth, and his angels were thrown down with him." Revelation 12:9 NASB

The devil is really good at "the blame game". He will convince you that everything is your fault and have you thinking "what if". I can't start to imagine how many times I did this to myself. I would say "maybe the reason is because I skipped a prenatal vitamin" or "if I hadn't walked around so long" (oh yeah, the devil had me thinking all types of crazy things/thoughts) or "I remember when I first found out I was pregnant I was moving out". Oh, and my favorite one "God must be punishing me for something I did before". In fact, it was simply part of God's master plan for my life. We can blame God but are we really willing to sit and think "God thoughts" about the situation? At the time that was hard for me to do. Consequently, it sent me into a place of depression and feeling "not good enough" to be blessed with my child.

We must get out of that frame of thinking. We don't know why God intervenes when He does, but I guarantee you that He has a plan for you. That outweighs the "self-pity" and "low self-esteem". Maybe God was saving me from some kind of pain that was far greater than the loss of my child. Maybe I would have died giving birth to her if I would have gone full term. Who knows? But that's how we need to start thinking. Thinking this way will ultimately get you out of your "dark place" and into the light. God truly has a plan for our lives and the sooner we recognize this and start to believe it, we will begin to understand it was a designed plan, not to hurt us but to keep us from despair.

Have you blamed yourself for things out of your control? What are situations you find the hardest to not take blame? When things don't go well or as we planned, blame is often one of the first emotions to be shared, most often we shift the blame to ourselves. What thing that is out of your control, do you blame yourself for? How do reconcile the validity with yourself?

Press Through

"You are from God, little children, and have overcome them; because greater is He who is in you than he who is in the world."
1 John 4:4 NASB

There were so many times I wanted to give up and throw in the towel. At times, I would stop going to church for certain periods of time then I would stop going all together for no particular reason. I went back to drinking and partying like I enjoyed it. To be honest, those things and places were not for me, and I was totally out of place. I wanted so many times to make the pain go away. I wanted to jump into bed, pull the curtains, and just sleep and hope that when I woke up it was all a horrible dream. But it wasn't a dream. It was reality. I had to see that and push through my hurt and pain. That meant I had to get up and pray. I had to encourage myself with His Holy Word (The Bible). I had to see the light at the end of the tunnel, no matter how dark it looked at the beginning. God told me to start doing things that I used to love doing. For me, that was basketball. When I played I felt relief? When I dribbled that ball, I would feel things being removed from my spirit that didn't belong there. I had to know that going through this and winning was my only option. I had to realize that this too shall pass. My dark place was not going to be my final place.

Doing this will not automatically take away all the pain. But, it will decrease some of your overall pain. And that's the place you start. You like sewing? Sew that sweater until your hearts content. You like cooking? Cook a Sunday dinner with all the fixings. Find your niche. Find your purpose from your pain. Find a gym and work out. Working out will surly help you relieve some pressure and stress that you have. Not only will you work off that stress, but you will feel good and have that summer body that you've always wanted. Go back and pick up that instrument that you set in the closet and play or dust off those wind pipes and sing again. Fall back in love with your passions. Serve at your church. BE an usher or in the choir. Remember what God told you to do and see those things through. Don't sit and let your time, talent, and treasure be wasted because you've given up. God needs you and deserves more from you. Give up on fighting it and bring that thing to pass. Trust me, you won't lose. God will bless and reward you mightily for your hard work and dedication to something. With God, anything is possible.

What do you find to be the thing that happens that causes you to recluse? What is a thing that happens to or around you that causes you to shut down? How do you get moving forward, again?

Make that Baby Proud

After I got over the grief of losing my daughter, I finally made it up in my head that I was going to make my baby proud. When I was pregnant I was in my last year of receiving my Associates degree in ECE (Early Childhood Education). To be specific, I was in my last quarter of graduating. When she passed I felt like I couldn't go on. I had made it this far and God had other plans for me. One day I looked up to heaven and cried. Then I said, "Baby mommy's going make you proud". I pressed through those classes. I talked and learned about babies who were born and alive and doing great. I was proud of myself that I could do that. It was not easy, but I made it. I had to dig to keep my mind from shifting from my newly found positive attitude and leave the negative. I kept thinking about how Jayla would feel if she was here and how I would want to be an example for her. I thought about her saying "if mommy can do it so can I". I also thought about her looking at me when I get to heaven and being proud that I am her mother and that I didn't give up. I know that if I had let my emotions get the best of me and not rely on God and thinking about how my daughter would have felt I wouldn't be where I am today. Every time I got up and took a test, went to class, or learned what I needed to know only took me closer and closer to my goals. I graduated with my graduating classes in 2010 as scheduled. Think about how your child would feel. Think about the impact you would have had on your child. That should be more than enough reason to keep moving. You can do it! Don't give up! God has so much more in store for you if you're obedient. It will happen! You will be blessed. Believe it and walk in it.

When you take the time to look at your life, now or where you have come from, what things would make your angel proud? What things are you proud to share with your angel?

Remember where they are!

""See that you do not despise one of these little ones, for I say to you that their angels in heaven continually see the face of My Father who is in heaven." Matthew 18:10 NASB

So, I know that babies go directly to Heaven no matter what. They are innocent and without sin. So, knowing that Jayla went straight to Heaven really helped me. As hard as it was to imagine not being with her I know for sure that she is in the best place that she could have ever been. She doesn't have to suffer any of the pains of this world would have brought her. She doesn't have to worry about bills, violence, or being broken hearted about anything. She is in a place where she will never experience any type of pain what so ever. That is so great to me when I think about it. I see her running down the street that is pathed with gold and worshipping God better than her mother could ever do. I see her telling God her thoughts and being ever so eloquent with her words to God and looking down on me and being proud of the person that I have become. No, I couldn't continue to be her mom but she is happy that I'm still here, standing, and believing God. My image of her is always amazing and powerful.

One other thing that gives me comfort is the fact that when I get to Heaven she will know me, and I will know her. I imagine that it will be as if we were never apart. We will be able to talk and walk together. She will be able to tell me her experiences being in Heaven and I will tell her mines when I was on earth. We will be in eternity together. If you don't know what eternity it is FOREVER. It's just like God to still be so merciful and great to us and let us have an opportunity to see our loved ones and babies, remembering that this time we won't have to worry about all of the bad things that could happens to them on this earthy ground. God makes it to where we will only know happiness the next time we meet. If that doesn't convince me to stay on a holy and righteous path, nothing will. I know I will see Jayla again and all of the sorrow and hurt that I felt when she left me in the natural will dissipate and I will find my love for my daughter for the rest of eternity in paradise.

What comforts you in your loss? Is it knowing that you loved one is no longer in pain? Is it knowing that you are only away from them for a period of time, not always?

You're Still a Mother!

""Can a woman forget her nursing child And have no compassion on the son of her womb? Even these may forget, but I will not forget you."Isaiah 49:15 NASB

Just like the scripture says, you will never forget your child. She or he is a part of you. Even though you may not have gotten a chance to raise that child, you are still a mother. When God blessed you with that seed in your body and fill the butterfly flutters, baby kicking, at conception you were officially a mother. I was and am a mother. People would say "you don't have a living baby" "or a miscarriage doesn't count as you having a baby". But that is just not true. When God put that seed into me, no matter how long I carried it, that ordained me as a mother. I remember one instance in my life when it was Mother's Day. We went to church and all of the mothers were going up and getting Mother's Day gifts. At the time, I was still mourning my daughter's death. So, I didn't want to go and get a gift because it hurt too bad. But my sisters convinced me to go up and get a gift because technically I was a mother. Reluctantly, I went up, because in my mind I was a mother. I had a C-section, my daughter was born, and she lived for 60 minutes. When I got up there the woman passing out the said "you're not a mother" and skipped right passed me. My family was very upset and at the end of the church service the person came to me and apologized to me and gave me a gift and we made amends. But my point is don't allow others to dictate who you are. When she said told me I wasn't a mother I was a little sad but at the end of the day I knew and still know that I am a mother. Nothing or no one has to convince me of that because I know what God told me and who I was blessed with even if it was for only 60 minutes. Plus, I have a social security card for her so that definitely makes it real (ha-ha). I still talk to my baby and do a small dedication to her on her birthday. I am a mother and I will always be one whether I have another child or not and so are you.

People often have their own selfish look of the world and even without knowing your story will make judgements and assumptions. What is the biggest incorrect judgement/ assumption, that someone has made about you?

Be Determined

"For I know the plans that I have for you,' declares the LORD, 'plans for welfare and not for calamity to give you a future and a hope." Jeremiah 29:11 NASB

At the time that I was dealing with Jayla's death my ex-boyfriend and I were taking care of my little sister. She was about to graduate high school. Now we had raised her for the last 2 years. We made sure she got on track, working on her self-esteem, and helped her to start getting good grades so she was able to graduate. It was truly a struggle, but by the grace of God she made it. When it was time for her to graduate, I was still in recovery mode. My body felt like I was not supposed to be there. But my mind had replayed all of the hard work we all put in to see that day and that she was successful, and I was determined to see it through. So, I got up, pain and all and saw my sister walk across that stage.

Whatever you are supposed to be doing before this tragedy happened be determined to see it through. Make it your mission to not let the things that bring you down consume and control your life. I can guarantee that if I would have stayed in that bed, even though I had every right to, I would have regretted it. Be determined to keep working on whatever your "it" is. Stay in church, be aware of what is going on around you because life will definitely have you and me in a world wind of emotions, thinking we are trapped. Don't be trapped, be determined.

What must you be determined, intentional about? What goals do you have to be determined to achieve even through your grief? It is never too late to achieve your goals and/or evaluate old goals and make new ones. What are some goals you really want to accomplish?

Remember God's Promises

"For by these He has granted to us His precious and magnificent promises, so that by them you may become partakers of the divine nature, having escaped the corruption that is in the world by lust."
2 Peter 1:4 NASB

When Jayla passed, I'm not going to lie, I thought everything that God promised me would no longer come to fruition. I thought that since this didn't happen, and knowing how much I wanted it, that maybe I didn't hear God clearly or something. Maybe the promises for me that God said He was going to do, wasn't for me and I heard them wrong. I was really tripping! So, in my human flesh, I started doubting everything in my life. I started lowering my expectations for my life. I started devaluing the things that were and still are going on in my life. I was here and alive when I could have bled out in the hospital. I still had my family who loved and supported me and drove me crazy (a good crazy, sometimes). I still had my nieces and nephews who would love up on me every single time I saw them. I didn't think about how blessed I was, because I thought of these things as "everyday things" or "things that I'm supposed to have". When the fact of the matter is we don't deserve any promises based on our lifestyles, but God grants us these things anyway. I had to change my thinking and realize what I did have vs what I didn't. When I did that my blessings truly outweighed what I didn't have or what I thought I should have.

So, for all of us we need to remember and wait for God's promises to come to our lives. God can't lie, and his promises are true, and it will come to pass. But we also have a part to play. Our minds and emotions and lack of faith can block our promises from coming forth. If you don't know what God has promised you get into a church were God leads you and where they are preaching biblical principles and truths. Some of his promises are that his love will never fail (I needed that one), that we can repent from sin and be forgiven, that He will bless those who delight themselves in his word, salvation to all that believe in His son. He will comfort us in our trials, and that He will finish the work that He started in us. These are just a few of them but the bible has so many more promises for us. So, no matter what your going through He will still do what He said He would do. The amazing thing is that these promises are rock solid, and He will never change them, and He is consistent. It's up to us to accept them and walk in them.

What promises have you made and not been able to keep? What promises were made to you and were never fulfilled? Which of God's promises do you challenge the most? What are you doing on your part to try him to fulfill His promises?

Renew Your Mind

"And do not be conformed to this world, but be transformed by the renewing of your mind, so that you may prove what the will of God is, that which is good and acceptable and perfect." Romans 12:2 NASB

My mind was most days my worst enemy. The thoughts that I was thinking about after Jayla passed were terrible and if I would have acted on them it would have been life altering and detrimental. I had to consistently change the way I thought in many cases and I am still working on it today. I remember thinking "maybe there isn't a God". That was a real thought for me. I quickly repented to God for that thought but that is what happens when we can't or won't renew our minds. For me, I'm very much a thinker. I don't usually say things until I've filtered all of the scenarios and reactions in my head. So, my mind is always working and sometime working overtime. I remember thinking "look at all these mothers who don't even want their children, but they have a bunch of them", or "look at her cussing her kids out. She or he don't deserve them". My mind was filled with anger at myself, God, and people that I didn't even know. I had no idea about their life, but I was judging them. I didn't want to help but instead I was judging them. I had lost Katrina in those times.

We have to learn how to cast down bad thoughts and replace them with positive ones. We have the ability to change our thoughts. It will be hard, but we can do it. Start thinking about what you have and what is currently important to you and about you. Start thinking the good in people, and if you're in a position, help them. Don't think bad thoughts about them. Think about how you can be a blessing. In my case, I could have helped those parents get the help that they needed. I know about parenting classes and programs that could help mothers, but I was so wrapped up in my own problems that I could not see what was in front of me. I now think the good in people and think of reasons and situations that could have landed them in the situations that they are in. Change your whole mind set and you will see the difference in how you look, how you feel, and the way you act. When you think you look good, no one can tell you that you don't. When you think you feel good you can do more things you desire for yourself instead of lying in bed. Perception and thought will do you good, but the question will always be *"what are you thinking?"*

What is your mind saying to your spirit? What is your mind believing that is harming your progress? How often do you make it a priority to renew your mind? What are you favorite ways to renew your mind?

57

Speak Life into Yourself

"But having the same spirit of faith, according to what is written, "I BELIEVED, THEREFORE I SPOKE," we also believe, therefore we also speak," 2 Corinthians 4:13 NASB

I had to learn on my journey how to speak life into myself. Often times someone would speak life into me and it blessed me tremendously, but I had to learn to do it for myself. People were not always around to keep me encouraged, so I had to do it myself. It was so hard to do but if I can be transparent, I started small. Instead of saying "it will never happen for me" I would say "why not me?". Instead of saying "I'm miserable today" I would say "today is a good day". The other part of it was that I had to learn, was to believe it. Saying it is only half the battle. When I started to believe it, I was a force to be reckoned with. I started to say, "I will have another baby and this one will live". I started to say "I can do all things through Christ that strengthens me (Philippians 4:13). That's how I also started to build up my spiritual muscles. I started to become bolder and bolder. They stopped being just something I said, those quotes became declarations. Then they became my life. I started to feel what I began to say. I knew that I was more than a conqueror (Romans 8:37). I knew I was worthy of more and I could give God and the ones around me more. I knew that when I speak things into my life those things would come forth. Just recently I made quotes and bible scriptures that resonated with me. I say them every day when I look in the mirror. Because I believe it, I see some of these things that I said come to pass.

It works. Start writing positive things about yourself and things that you want for yourself. Start to say them daily until you start to believe it. If need be say them hourly. The things that we say and BELIEVE will come to pass. Don't let the negatives come out of your mouth. I know that it is easier to speak negative but will yourself and step out of that 'woe is me' and get some HOLY BOLDNESS. Speak the things that you don't even believe yet. Trust me, if you continue to say it you won't have a choice but to start believing it. God will grant your desires just speak them to Him.

What are things that you speak negatively about yourself? What are some small things that you can change to a more positive declaration? What is it you doubt you can achieve? Do you believe you have the power to change your situation?

Speak things into Existence

"Death and life are in the power of the tongue, and those who love it will eat its fruit."
Proverbs 18:21 NASB

Going deeper with speaking, I had to also speak things into existence for my life. I told you when Jayla initially died I thought life was over and there was no point in living or holding on to dreams at all. So, I had to work hard at speaking until it manifested or the situation worked out. This was the best way I could get out of my funk. My Pastor Darren Thomas once preached that we needed to "bind" and "loose" things and situations to our lives. He also talked about how we are always "binding the devil", but we also can "bind" things to ourselves. So, I started "binding" hope, peace, and longevity to my life. I "loosed" the things that I was supposed to be doing in the atmosphere like building on my dreams. I started to do what God had for me to do in his kingdom. I am no longer letting my time, talent, and treasure lie dormant. I won't grow if I do. I've waited long enough and the things that I'm supposed to do will come out of me!

Growing is hard but it is harder to live with the regret and shame of not doing what God has told us to do. Reconsider giving up. Bind a hope and a future to your life. Loose a great life for yourself and your family. Don't give up because the reward will be great. I am suggesting these things because I had to do them to keep my sanity. And it works! God put these things in His word not to fill up a book, but to tell us what to do in situations like this. Speak whatever your "it" is. You define what it is for your life and speak that thing into existence. You will enjoy your life and the fruits of it if you do.

What do you want to come to you that you need to speak into the atmosphere? What do you desire that you have not spoken? Do you understand that God gives you the power to speak things into your life? In the same regards, if you speak negative, it is working against you?

Have Faith

"And Jesus answered saying to them, "Have faith in God. Truly I say to you, whoever says to this mountain, 'Be taken up and cast into the sea,' and does not doubt in his heart, but believes that what he says is going to happen, it will be granted him. Therefore I say to you, all things for which you pray and ask, believe that you have received them, and they will be granted you." Mark 11:22-24 NASB

Faith is more than just saying "I believe." I had to maximize my faith during this hardship. With all that was going on I had to know that what God said to me was true. In an illustration shown to us by Pastor Darren Thomas, he carried a heavy chair on his back while walking and he said we must know that the things that God said will happen even in the mist of our problems. That means even if we have to cry and carry that problem, faith tells us that it won't be long before the problem will be lifted. My problem was that I wanted her and believing that it wouldn't be a second chance for me. But, still to this day I have faith that I will have a baby. The thing that I know now that I didn't know before was that God had and has more in store for me before that can happen. I'm ok with that. I have faith (without having to see it and not knowing where in the world it is coming from) that He has it under control and He can't and won't lie to me.

Please I urge you to have faith. It may look like it's not going to happen, but it will. Don't look at the situation as it is now. Get your spiritual goggles and see your life how God sees it. If you can imagine it then increase it by 1,000 because we can't even image what God has in store for us if we keep the faith and do His will. Now look at God. If we only do the minimum God will max it in a way that is unimaginable. Go through your struggle with hope and be strategic in your thought pattern for your life. God will increase you.

What do have a challenge believing is possible? Having a child? Getting married? Be healed? What do you honestly doubt God can do? Is there anything God can't do?

Rediscover You

"I will give thanks to You, for I am fearfully and wonderfully made; Wonderful are Your works, And my soul knows it very well." Psalms 139:14 NASB

There were a couple of times when I had to rediscover myself. The things that I set out to do didn't have the same feeling and I felt like I was sinking. I didn't have that same fulfillment that I once had. So, I really thought about what I wanted and the trajectory of my life. I started to try new things and go places that were foreign to me. I had to step out of my comfort zone. Doing that made me see things I've never seen and do things that I've never done. It was easy for me to stay at home and just do the things that were "safe". Sometimes the path to healing leads you to some good and unknown places. I was able to meet people that I wouldn't have talked to normally and learn insight from their lives. Sometimes we think that we are the only people going through something and that is far from the truth. When I started to open up more I learned that other people have went through the same thing that I had. I was able to learn constructive ways of handling my emotions, my health, and my overall wellbeing.

Go out with the intentions of learning or meeting someone new. Get to know them and learn from them. They may have methods that will work for you that you never thought of. Don't discount someone because they seem to "have it all together". You never know, they might have been worse off than you. Take time to see why people come into your life and don't let your opinion or bias deter you. Rediscovering yourself does not mean that you completely give up on your entire being but think about other things that will make your life more meaningful. Get a hobby outside of your normality. Work on something that you had a brief thought about, but you never really acted on it. The choice is yours and only you have the ability to do it.

What are some things you lost in transition while dealing with your loss? What are somethings you want to find joy in again? Are you willing to step out of you comfort zone? Are you will to change your surroundings to be a better version of you?

Don't let the devil steal your joy!
"Consider it all joy, my brethren, when you encounter various trials," James 1:2 NASB

That devil loves to kill joy. He hates when you have joy so he will do everything in his power to take it. I let him take my joy and to be all the way honest, I let him take it a couple of times. I would have high days then I would have low days. I was never consistent or content. On my high days, I felt like I could conquer anything and on my low days… oh man, watch out. I was moody and irritable at everything and at nothing. I would stay like this for days and everyone could see the difference. At the time, I don't think I saw it but looking back, I definitely do. I let the devil take me on an emotional roller coaster that I never wanted to be on. But the key word was "I" let him do these things. If I would have made up my mind and made a conscious effort to change my attitude the devil wouldn't have been able to change my mood and steal my joy. It was not easy, and I still struggle with it sometimes but I intentionally think on things that are good, lovely, and be of a good report (Philippians 4:8).

Once we change our attitudes and think the way God wants us to think the devil won't be able to bother us with that anymore no matter how hard he tries. He won't be able to steal our joy. Now, he will try to hurt us in other areas, but we will conquer those things as well. As hard as it may be, you must keep trying and pushing to be joyful. The devil won't give up because his primary focus is to kill our soul and the rest will be easy if he gets our souls. You can fight, and you will win. This thing will be a war that must be fought daily but once you obtain your goal you will win this war. Stick with God and ask him to help you defeat this war.

Command your angels (all 72,000 angels that you have) to guard your mind. A prayer that I learned from my pastor is to ask God to keep Satan off our radar, so he won't be able to find us. Pray that prayer into your body where you find you joy is lacking, and God will increase it and make the devil leave your joy alone. If you fight you will surly win. Fight for it because it's worth it.

What are some things you want to find joy in again? What changes in your attitude can you make now? Do you tend to surround yourself with positive, joyful people? If no, do you have some you can start surrounding yourself with? Do you believe misery loves company?

Don't hide behind your family

Anybody who knows me knows I LOVE my family. I will put their needs before mine in a heartbeat. While I was going through this situation my family was a double-edged sword. The crazy part was that if wasn't their fault. I used them as a crutch. When I didn't want to deal with my thoughts, I would invite them over. I knew I was supposed to be dealing with my emotional state, but I choose to avoid it. They would come over and it would be all good until I was alone again. Those thoughts that hunted me didn't leave, they were just pushed in the back of my mind. And sure, enough they came back and sometimes they came even harder. I was naive to think that a momentary action would erase all the bad thoughts I was thinking. So, I would try it again. I would go over their houses this time to run away from them (I'm not sure why I thought it would be different just because I went to them instead of them coming to me). Once again it left me in the same predicament. After all the fun was over I felt that emptiness again. I would have been in a never-ending cycle if I hadn't broken it with the help of God. I eventually had to stop running, face my pain and break it. When I did it felt so liberating.

I want you to know how it feels to be liberated. Don't hide and bury yourself in mom, dad, sisters, brothers, nieces, nephews, or anyone else. They can't heal you. They can help you heal but the ultimate healing is up to you and with God's help. But you have to be willing to get the help and comfort in places that you rather not. Don't be like me and use your family as an invisible crutch, leaning on them when you should have been leaning on God. If you do a little God will bless your little.

Who are you leaning on that only provides temporary distraction? How will stop the never ending cycle? Do you feel like you are supported in your family or more from friends?

Only the Strong Survive?

"And He has said to me, "My grace is sufficient for you, for power is perfected in weakness." Most gladly, therefore, I will rather boast about my weaknesses, so that the power of Christ may dwell in me." 2 Corinthians 12:9 NASB

I've heard that slogan "only the strong survive" so many times, contrary to popular belief, in my situation that did not apply. When I lost Jayla, I was weakened. I was broken. Nothing was "strong" about me. I let my emotions control my mood and attitude. That quote definitely didn't pertain to me. But guess what? I'm here and I survived. Even in my brokenness I still survived. Although I lost a few battles ultimately, I won the war. In my weakness, God was able to build me up again. I was able to stand brave and honest about my feelings with God. God honored that and cleansed me from the inside out. I feel that He was only able to do this because of my vulnerability. If I was "strong" then that would have just been a mask to cover all the doubt and issues going on with me.

We don't always have to be "strong" to survive. God wants us to be honest first off to even start to move into the direction of healing. Being completely alone with God and crying out to him is not weak. It is a place of opening and letting the real you out, so God can start to mend the broken places in you. God can do all things, but he won't if you are showing a "fake" you. He gives us the opportunity to open up freely to him. He doesn't make us do anything, even if it's in our best interest or in his will. He needs a willing vessel and that's us. When I say be vulnerable to God, I'm not saying to play the victim role or "woe is me" card but bring God the realist version of you that you can. God will bless it and He will honor it. Like a member of my church, Angela Tyler said "BE

BRAVE, BE BOLD, and BE BIG." God will accept the best you if you give it to him.

Are you afraid to show and or admit your weaknesses? If yes, why? If no, is it because you feel you have none? Have you ever had a situation you expected you would be strong, but really should have been vulnerable? Was there anyone there to make sure you were okay? Has anyone ever told you not to cry? How did you handle that? Did you feel your feelings were not being validated? Did you make your feelings known?

Remember what you wanted

""These things I have spoken to you while abiding with you."
John 14:25 NASB

When I was a child I prayed to God. I prayed about what kind of family I wanted, how I wanted my kids to be reared, and how I wanted to be married before I had kids. As a matter of fact, I prayed to God and said I wanted to be a virgin when I got married. As I got older and grown I forgot about these things. Although I asked for forgiveness, I wasn't married before I had an intimate encounter with a man and I wasn't married before I got pregnant with Jayla. In all of my sin, God never forgot. God knew that while Jayla would have been well taken care of, it was never my desire to be a mother without a husband. I would have felt like I failed my child because I wanted more for her than I had for myself. I wanted her to be raised in a two-parent household and as a whole family, not co-parenting or having to make arrangements. So maybe God didn't give me her because of what I wanted. He also knew that when He took her I would eventually be ok. God knew how I would feel in the long run even though I would have loved and cared for Jayla.

Remember the things that you wanted from God. Remember the goals and dreams that you wanted to accomplish for your life. Things that happen is not always bad and to do you harm. God remembered even when we didn't. Let this time be a time of reigniting the things that you wanted or the way you wanted to do it. Believe that this is a way, even in sadness and hurt, to continue what you stopped because you found out that you were pregnant. Be purpose driven. Cause your hurt and pain to be passion and desire to do what God has called you to do or to be. God still desires those things that are in you to be birthed out of you. Show God that you remember and that those things will indeed come to pass. Make God smile upon the faces of His holy and true people.

What did you want before your grief derailed your joy? What desires do you have that can still go forth, even now? What desires have allowed to be lost in the fog?

The Transition

34 You yourselves know that these hands ministered to my own needs and to the men who were with me. 35 In everything I showed you that by working hard in this manner you must help the weak and remember the words of the Lord Jesus, that He Himself said, 'It is more blessed to give than to receive.'" Acts 20:34-35 NASB

There is a reason during the flight attendant's safety presentation, at the beginning of every flight, they say "In the event of a decrease in cabin pressure oxygen masks will drop from overhead. Put on your mask, secure it, extend the tube, the bag will not inflate, but oxygen is flowing. Then help someone who may need assistance, "*but why? Why wouldn't I make sure my child is secure first?* I always put the needs of others before my own." Here is why, if you secure you child's mask first, you may be too oxygen deprived, and not have the time or strength to get your own mask on before you pass out. On the other hand, if your mask is secure then you have full use of all your faculties, now able to assist others who may not be able to help themselves. God is often be the oxygen mask, you may not see a visual indicator that He is there and working, but He is always working for your good.

We who take care of others must be diligent and intentional to make self-care a priority! You may ask *"what does that look like?"* Well each person is different, and the needs of each person are different. So, ask yourself "what does it look like for me to feel taken care of, at my best, healthy and whole (or at least on the right path).

At this point in Katrina's story it transitions from her hurt and the changes in the trajectory of her path towards God and moves to the point of tips, advice and encouragement to help you get unstuck and start pressing forward. This is also the point in the journey that you get to look at how you can change your current circumstances and press through to the best you.

How can you truly care for others properly if you're running on fumes? Take care of yourself, be good to yourself and love others as Christ has been the example for us all.

Why do we put the needs of others before our own? Why do we make doing for, treating and pampering ourselves less important doing those things for others? Is it that we don't love our selves enough, or do we just desire to show love to those we care about and care for more?

Love Yourself

"He who gets wisdom loves his own soul; He who keeps understanding will find good." Proverbs 19:8 NASB

Loving myself after Jayla passed was hard. I had no self-worth. I let myself go and I didn't care. I barely wanted to leave the house because I didn't want anyone to even love me. I was so good at loving but inside my self-love was so miniature. At that point, I had no idea how to love myself. I over achieved in some things because I felt my best was not good enough. When I looked in the mirror I didn't see a person who was worthy of love. This ordeal messed with my mind so bad. I had to reteach myself how to love me again.

First, I found out what love was (1 Corinthians 13:4-7). God had to be the first source that I went to. Then I started to talk to myself about what is good and lovely about myself. I started to remove what I could "bring to the table". I went to the gym and stopped looking at myself as unlovable. It wasn't easy, and I still struggle with that a bit, but it takes time. I was able to show myself what God saw in me then for my future. I was and am what God said I am. Therefore, I started to treat myself with the love and self-worth that I treated everyone else with.

If we don't love ourselves no one else will. People will treat us the way we treat ourselves. And if we don't love ourselves we will think we deserve to be mistreated. Find out what is great and lovely about **you**. As you begin to know, start to act like that version of yourself. Don't self-sabotage. The world will try to do those things to you. If you have absolutely no idea where to start say: I AM BEAUTIFUL, I AM GREAT, I AM MORE THAN

ENOUGH, I AM GOD'S CHOSEN, I AM GODS ANNOINTED. If you believe you can, you are half of the way there. Picture the love you have for yourself and work hard to obtain that love for yourself. I believe that you can do it. Change your emotional outcome but inputting positivity.

How do you love yourself? How do you demonstrate self-love, so others may know how to love you? Do you know your love language? Want to find out? Go Here!
https://www.5lovelanguages.com

Prune Unproductivity

"Every branch in Me that does not bear fruit, He takes away; and every branch that bears fruit, He prunes it so that it may bear more fruit." John 15:2 NASB

I was so unproductive when I was dealing with my daughter's death. I literally wasn't doing anything. I acted as if God hadn't given me an assignment to do or play a part in anyone's life. I always had the natural ability to listen to people and their problems. I can listen to the whole story and give wisdom based on my experiences. I was unable to do that at that time because I was too fragile. I was so busy talking about myself and how it was not fair about my daughter that people were unable to talk to me like they used to be able to. I had taken a God given ability and reversed it. Now I wasn't just talking about the situation, I was complaining. Complaining is counterproductive. I needed to stop that and soon. Because if I didn't it would have become a part of me. I had to really dig down and pray myself out of unproductivity.

What have you noticed that you have been unproductive in? Are there things that you know you are good at, just sitting on your mental desk? When you think of how you were before the tragedy is your life better or worse? Think about these thinks and erase counter productivity from yourself. I know it hurts and that your heart is broken, but if you're living a life of productivity God will bless it. Do something and show the devil that he can't take something that God gave you in the first place. You are alive and well and God still expects you to produce what he has given you. You can be productive whether you are happy or sad. It is a state of mind and you have the ability to control it. Make a vow to yourself and God to keep being productive in your home, life, and ministry. Prune unproductivity from your life.

What do you do that hinders your ability to move forward? What current habits and/or activities do you do that feeds into your ability to avoid your progress forward? Idle Hands – what can you start doing to use up some of your "free time"?

Expect Greatness

"May You increase my greatness And turn to comfort me."
Psalms 71:21 NASB

My mind frame when Jayla passes was "bad things always happen to me". I was soaking in self-pity. I didn't expect greatness in any area of my life. My new moto was "oh well, what will happen will happen". In that moment, I was creating my future. I was speaking the wrong things into the atmosphere and that was exactly what I was getting. I got what I expected when I finally switched my thoughts with the help of some wise people I started to expect greatness. I started to know that what I thought and sought out to do will truly come to pass. I was a new person with new aspirations and a totally different perspective on how to accomplish things that I wanted to work towards. Now I know that I can do all things that I set my mind to. I know that greatness will come from me and it will truly be a work of art.

The bible says that life and death is in the power of the tongue (Proverbs 18:21). So, you can damage your future just by what comes from your mouth especially when it comes to your greatness (success). God wont over-ride our self-proclaimed declarations that come from you. Start saying and speaking greatness from each area in your life. When you do these things, you will begin to see your life change. Think greatness and greatness will come from you. God wants to hear your declarations, so He can bless you. He already knows your greatness, but He is waiting for you to start to see it and walk in it. You are destined for it and God wrote it in His plan for you. You can be all that God says you are but also who you say you are. What will you say about yourself? What do you expect in your today and in your future? Think about it, write it down, and start to walk in greatness.

What do you expect from yourself? What goals are you sure you will achieve? How do you plan for great outcomes?

Take Care of You

"Or do you not know that your body is a temple of the Holy Spirit who is in you, whom you have from God, and that you are not your own? For you have been bought with a price: therefore, glorify God in your body." 1 Corinthians 6:19-20 NASB

Before I found out I was pregnant I was at the gym and working on my body. I had the mentality of whole wellness. I watched what I ate, what I did, and how much sleep I got. After I got pregnant I was still trying to eat well, take prenatal vitamins, and do doctor approved exercises. But after she passed I completely just stopped everything. I gained weight and over indulged in food. I ate what I wanted and did nothing for a workout. I wasn't even working out my mind because I didn't pick up a book or even a Bible. I wasn't thinking of the things that God had for me. Food for me didn't take the pain away but it gave me something to do. I was too depressed to do anything. I was drinking and all. I was doing serious damage to my body. Technically, it was abuse to my body. I wasn't doing anything to improve the overall quality of my life. The moment I finally started to change was when our first lady Sonya Thomas came to me and told me that we needed to be whole to operate properly in the kingdom of God. She also encouraged me to start taking care of myself and change the way I dressed, and it will change the way I think about myself.

If you look good, you will feel good and vice versa. Our body is the temple of the Holy Spirit. This means God wants us to be the very best and heathiest version of ourselves. Don't indulge like I did for absolutely no reason. We need to be healthy to be able to be a complete vessel for God. He doesn't want us to just talk about His word, but to also be healthy so we can live a long time and let people see the shine of God in our lives. Start small. Go to the gym 2 or 3 times a week. Put the pop down and get a water instead. Bake that chicken instead of frying it. Go home and cook something healthy instead of eating out. While you're watching TV do some crunches. The little changes you make will help you to accomplish realistic goals. And guess what, once you start it won't go anywhere but up. The choice is yours and you can do it.

How do you take care of yourself? Do you tend to take care of others over yourself? When was the last time you did something to take care of you?

Comfort Someone Else

""Comfort, O comfort My people," says your God." Isaiah 40:1 NASB

When I was going through I thought no one understood me. I thought I was the only person going through this. "Surly, no one else had the same struggle" was my thought. Oh, how wrong I was. I met about 3 or 4 moms that had been through the same thing or something very similar. Thankfully, I was in my stages of healing when I met them or when it happened. I was able to comfort them and talk to them. I was able to give them advice as well. I was able to tell them some of the feelings of hurt and regrets that they may have because I had them. I was able to encourage them and tell them to keep standing and keep moving. I was able to pray for them in a specific way because I knew the hurt and enormous pain that they were going through. I told one woman to not live in fear and the thoughts she was having was a trick of the enemy. I explained that he put those thoughts in her head, so she would never heal. I (with God's guidance) was able to remove her from some of the darkness and depression that I went through before she got there. I'm still able to talk to people and to be a listening ear or a shoulder to cry on because while others are saying "oh I can imagine" it was our reality and I could relate. I could also tell the with boldness "I MADE IT" and so can you.

In situations like this, most of the time people wants to talk to someone who had been through it and LIVED through it. I know I would have wanted that. Be that person for someone. Tell them they will live and not die. Tell them that God is still with them. Tell them it's not their fault. Let them know that God still has a calling on their lives. Be that shoulder to cry on and that listening ear. It does wonders for people. Don't hold your wisdom in. You never know, your encouraging words may be the difference between life and death. Show someone that there is a way out. Be someone's rescue on earth. God gives us experiences and knowledge not to keep it bottled up, but to advance His kingdom. If you don't think comforting someone is a part of God's kingdom it is. So, advance His kingdom.

Do you encounter people who are hurting? Do you encounter people who are experiencing something worse that you or something you may have overcome? Are you too wrapped in your own pain that you are no help for anyone?

Don't Let Pity Control You

"Casting all your anxiety on Him, because He cares for you."
1 Peter 5:7 NASB

One thing I vowed to myself is to not be pitiful, again. I did that for too long with the passing of Jayla. I thought of myself as pathetic. Here I was surrounded by healthy born kids all around me and I couldn't get the job done, so to speak. I was hard on myself. There was plenty of times when I just shut down completely. No one could talk to me or anything. I was in a bad head space. At this point it was up to me to make a change. If I didn't want to change my frame of reference no one else would have been able to get thorough to me. I had to take that self-pity from my back and replace it with love and acceptance. I also couldn't see what it was doing to me. People with spiritual sensitivity could see that I was depressed, had low self-esteem, and that I wasn't sure about myself. But I was so deep in it that I literally didn't see it and wondered why people that prayed with me would pray that spirit away. I was too close to it and made it an everyday part of myself. When I finally told myself that I wasn't going to be like that anymore I was finally liberated. I was on my way to healing.

Are you up one day and down the next? When you go around people do they constantly ask you "what's wrong" but you feel perfectly fine? Those were the things that were happening to me. First, try understanding what is happening in your mind, that you may be completely unaware. Take these things into consideration when people are always asking you if you are ok. Then start to do things that will help you get out of self-pity. I would urge you to pray to God to reveal to you what you are feeling so you can deal with it first. The (the hard part) do it. It will help you. If not, you will continue to put undue stress and strain on your mind, soul, spirit, and body. Go back to the original you. Open up and start to repair yourself. Give your broken places to God and He will substitute them with His love and glory.

Do you pity yourself? Do you compare yourself with other people you feel are doing better than you it brings you down emotionally or you beat yourself up?

Be True to Yourself

"and you will know the truth, and the truth will make you free." John 8:32 NASB

For a long time, I could honestly say I wore a mask. I was not the real and genuine me. I lost myself in this hard and trying time. Before this point of my daughter's death I knew what, I wanted in life and who I was (mostly). I was happy and so looking forward to my future. Any amount of progress (small or large), would get me excited. After that time, I was lucky if I wanted to get out of bed and take a shower. I wasn't any good to anyone because I wasn't good for myself. I had to finally bring back the old Trina and learn the core values and principles that I lived by that brought me happiness. Thank God I could get it back because sometimes it's hard. I love the me that I am, now and I'm enjoying the new things that God has for me.

Don't let situations and circumstances (as hard as they may be), tear you down from the inside out. It will get better and you will remember what you loved about yourself. Go back to that and be your original self. You can't be someone else so stop looking at what other people have or who they have and focus on you. I know that it will be hard but with a lot of fasting and praying you will get through it. Don't give up and don't throw in the towel. God has amazingness in store for you. He didn't leave you then and He never will. Focus on you and the rest will fall into place. Begin a new thing and revive an old one. It will work, and you will surely be blessed.

Do you know who you are? Do you like who you are? Do you

change things about yourself to fit in? What do you like? Do your statements begin with "Mr. Blank said…" or "They say…"? On what authority do they have to say…? What do "you say"?

Be Hopeful*

""Oh that my request might come to pass, and that God would grant my longing!" Job 6:8 NASB

To this day, I still have hope that I will become a mommy. When I say hope I'm not talking about crying, I don't know if it's going to happen, hope. I'm talking about that hope the I believe it will truly happen. While I'm hopeful I'm preparing myself for the child that will come to me. So, I take care of my temple the best I can (no smoking and drinking) to make sure I'm able to produce a child. I'm also getting my mind ready to become responsible for a human being that God entrusted into my care and who will have demanding needs. In know that God will grant the desire of my heart. Standing strong in hope helps me to not get down on myself and have pity parties. I know that God will do it.

My pastor Darren Thomas talked about being hopeful in a Sunday morning service at church. Show God that you believe in what He said. It will come to pass. Continue to hope for it. You can't let what happened stop your hope. God will show himself strong. He will sow a new thing in your life. Hope for what you know will happen. I promise God will do it for you. I learned that God can only do something if you believe and hope. God said he will show up and show up bigger than you could have ever imagined. Just say "God I HOPE so" and believe what your spirit and soul says about your situation. It is vital to your success to cover yourself in hope and belief of God.

What are some things in your life that you are hopeful, God will fulfill? Does it involve relationships? Does it involve your education? Does it involve your career? What gives you hope? In the state of the world today does it make you feel hopeless?

Go Forward

"Brethren, I do not regard myself as having laid hold of it yet; but one thing I do: forgetting what lies behind and reaching forward to what lies ahead," Philippians 3:13 NASB

Will I ever forget about Jayla? Of course not, but I had to move forward if I wanted to have any type of life. If I lived in defeat and anger nothing would come forth from me. I had to show the devil that he would not continue to have control over me. Once you heal and you are ready again to have a baby, do it and have fun (for married people only). I vowed to myself that when I was married that I wouldn't be afraid to have another baby. Be hungry for what you want. I had to do it.

One Sunday my assistant pastor Cheryl Thomas talked about "No more dry bones". We must go forward to not experience dry bones in our lives. Like I said we will not forget about our child/children who are in heaven. That would be foolish to believe that, just don't be in fear to try again. Dare to dream and make it come into fruition. God will restore. God will give you more than you ever imagined. Receive from God and do it in a spirit of determination and action. Move forward, move forward, move forward.

Do you spend a lot of time looking at your past? Do you spend so much time looking back that you miss the good things right in front of you? What is the first thing you need to do to show progress forward? Are you stuck with "dry bones"?

Be Transparent

"Therefore, laying aside falsehood, SPEAK TRUTH EACH ONE of you WITH HIS NEIGHBOR, for we are members of one another." Ephesians 4:25 NASB

As I'm writing this book I'm speaking from a place of healing. I can see things clearly now. If I would have written this book when I was going through my situation I probably wouldn't have been all the way honest. I may not even have had experienced all that God needed me to experience so I could stand as a witness of His greatness. Now I can be very transparent when it comes to me telling my story and being a support for someone else. I couldn't talk to anyone if I wasn't healed because I still would have had thought and actions that would have been contradictory to what I was speaking out of my mouth. I can now produce the purpose that God intended this book to be. As she was encouraging me to write this book Pastor Cheryl told me "you know when you are strong enough to write this when you don't cry anymore". That spoke volumes to me. I was finally at that point. I can talk about everything that happened to me, every emotion, every thought, every mood and do it without crying or breaking down. I can talk to anyone now and not go into hiding for days because I'm depressed all over again. I bless God that I'm not in that place anymore.

A couple of chapters ago in this book I talked about helping someone else. You cannot do it without being transparent. People can tell if you are being fake. Transparency is a must if you want to make a breakthrough in someone's life. If you haven't healed or your still mad at God or anyone else people will see and recognize that and at that moment you shouldn't be ministering to anyone because you don't even believe what you are saying, if you do that people will begin to not trust you. When you really commit, and be a light for someone in honesty, God will bless you and someone will be able to heal because of your transparent nature. Be a mentor and an example of letting go of the pressure and let God take away that burden. And guess what? If you do this, before you even open your mouth, people will see that you are a real person and they will be able to trust you.

Are you open? Do you only say what you feel and/or think? If you were asked the same questions by five different people would your answers be the same? Can people depend on you to be honest? Do you allow yourself to be vulnerable for the sake of progress and healing?

Thank God for Restoration

"Restore to me the joy of Your salvation and sustain me with a willing spirit." Psalms 51:12 NASB

For me, restoration used to be a bad word. That meant you did something so terrible and God needed to "restore you" and you would be forgiven. It wasn't until this situation and pastor Darren started speaking restoration in every area of my life that I understood the real definition. My daughter, the one that I had dreams and aspirations for was gone and in my mind all things were dead. I had to get my mind restored first because nothing will happen if I still had the same mind set. Then I had to get my heart restored from all the feelings that I had let fester in it. It was almost like I had taken my brain and heart out of my head and chest, laid it at the altar, and let God rebuild and renew it into what His original plan and design was for my life. After that I had to keep it from forming up again. When God restored me I literally felt like a new person.

When being restored, be careful not to let the things that you have been restored from come back. The devil has a way of having us remember what God has already brought us out of. Be restored in your mind, body, soul, and spirit, go forward and don't look back. As humans, we can easily revert to our normal habits of depression and low self-esteem. But, I learned to not have low self-esteem you have to get out of "self" and let God restore you and give you all that you lack. Therefore, let God restore to you all that the devil, life, or yourself have taken from you and "Thank God for His restoration".

What do you need to have restored? Do you like Katrina need your mind restored first to change your mind set before you can have anything else restored? What are you holding back from God, which He can restore, if you let Him?

They don't understand, but they understand

"Consider what I say, for the Lord will give you understanding in everything." 2 Timothy 2:7 NASB

I would get so mad when someone would say "I understand what you're going through" when they had never been through it. People who had their beautiful babies and children had no right to say that in my opinion (my old opinion). I would say "how could they possibly understand what I'm going through?". I would even go as far as to say "look at her. She doesn't even want her kids". "Why didn't God just give me her kids". I now know that is was totally the wrong attitude. I had to really wrap my mind around understanding what they were saying. Once I got it I stopped getting mad and having evil thoughts.

Even though some of the people that were saying that had not gone through what I had they felt my hurt. They felt my pain. They saw the things that I was going through, and it hurt them because a person that they loved, had a relationship, or even a friendship with was hurting. They empathized with me. They understood and shared my feelings. The next time someone says, "I understand how you feel", it may not be the physical pain, but they can feel your emotional and, in some cases, spiritual pain. Also, you have to understand that Jayla and your baby had grandparents, aunts, uncles, cousins, etc. that had plans of meeting and building relationships with your baby. They feel the hurt and devastation of not being able to see their love one. So, the next time you encounter that situation think on this and understand that they are truly hurt because you are hurt.

Do you feel many times people don't get it, don't get you? Do you feel what you are going through it is impossible for others to understand? Do you feel you are all alone in your pain? Do you understand that you are not alone? Have you ever felt someone else's pain? Have you ever been able to empathize with other people's pain?

Don't Give up on God

"'Do not fear, for I am with you; Do not anxiously look about you, for I am your God. I will strengthen you, surely I will help you, Surely I will uphold you with My righteous right hand.'" Isaiah 41:10 NASB

There were times where I just wanted to break down and give up on God. I wanted to completely remove myself from God. I felt like God didn't love me and there was no reason to keep serving him. I was so depressed and stressed. I had no self-worth about myself. I would tell other people that they could make it, but I didn't believe it for myself. I'm a very internal person so I didn't just come straight out and tell God and the people around me that I was throwing in the towel. But in my mind, it was a completely different story. I honestly believed that life was over and there was no coming back. I was damaging myself and when I eventually realized that I had to go repent to God and show Him that I still trusted Him. I had to see that even though my baby was gone, I was still here, and I have a promise on my life and I had things to do. Only God could have shown me that because I wasn't able to see it for myself. I still was healthy, I had my family that loved and supported me, and most of all I still had God. When I was denying God, He could have thrown me to the wolves to be devoured but He didn't give up on me. If He didn't through all of this, how dare I give up on Him.

No matter how bad you feel remember God will never give up on us. Even when we choose to stop believing it He will continue to love us unconditionally and when you ask for him and repent He will always be there for us. He will repair your heart. He will be your redeemer, He will fill the void in your life. He will never give up or throw us aside. He is our father and He loves us. Go back and trust Him again and He will show up as never before. How do I know? Because I've been through it and I'm a living testimony.

Do you understand God is always there for you? Do you understand that even in your pain he is working for your good? Do you think God makes bad things happen? He is punishing you? Although sometimes things may happen that are parts of your testimony? Could you understand good times if you never experience bad times?

Pray to God

"Seek the LORD and His strength; Seek His face continually." 1 Chronicles 16:11 NASB

Prayer was vital in this situation. I didn't know why this happened to me and no one did. The doctors didn't know or give me an explanation either. All they could tell me was "sometimes these things happen". So, I had to get answers from the only person who knew. I had to pray and lay out before the Lord to get the answer. After praying I believe that some of the things that I mentioned in previous chapters were the reasons. After I got the answers I was still left with a broken heart. Therefore, I had to go back to God in prayer, but this time to fix the problems that I was having. As I continued to pray God was giving me peace. Not the peace that only lasted until I stopped praying, but the peace that made me feel that I could live through it. Then when I prayed more and more I noticed that my prayers were starting to sound different. Instead of just praying for myself, I stared praying for people who had experienced the same trauma. I started to intercede for my family that they always had healthy babies and never had to experience this. My whole prayer was so different, and I was grateful that God revealed that to me.

Prayer truly changed things. Don't ever think that God is not hearing your prayers. If you go to Him sincerely He will honor and accept that prayer. Start praying for people who have experienced lost as I did. Start praying for your mind to change and that you will be totally healed. If you continue to pray without ceasing things will look different. You will have a totally different perspective and will be able to process it. God will start to speak through you as you pray, telling you the things to pray for. If you continue to make your needs and those around you known to God, He won't have any other choice but to bless you. You will begin with questions about why this has happened to you and before you know it you will start to change questions into declarations and decrees as you increase your time in prayer with God. He will start to reveal things to you and change up your prayer style. Don't stop praying.

Do you pray? Do you pray only to request from God? Do you pray prayers of thanks, for things other than your meals? Do you say grace over meals or just dig in? Do you feel unworthy of direct communication with God?

God knew who to Trust

""Before I formed you in the womb I knew you, And before you were born I consecrated you; I have appointed you a prophet to the nations." Jeremiah 1:5 NASB

Although, this was a traumatic experience for me God knew that I would make it. Even when I didn't believe it, or the devil was putting things in my ear, God never doubted that I could make it. He never puts more on you than you can bear, and He knew that I wouldn't do something foolish like take my life or hurt myself beyond where I could rebound from (even though I had thoughts). He knew I wouldn't lose my mind forever. He knows that I wouldn't end up in an institution. He knew He could trust me to handle the situation. I promise I thought it was over, but God had other plans for me.

I know this is hard to deal with, but God knows you can handle it. This too shall pass, and you will be on the other side victorious. Trust God as much as he trusts in you. Know that, life as you know it is not over. It is not over, and the bottom will not fall out from under you. You will make it and God will prove to you that His word is true, and He will never forsake you.

Who do you trust? Who do you put your faith in? In what situations do you put your trust and faith in? Can God trust you? Do you feel trust is earned not given or given not earned? Trust equals faith…

Feed Me (Studying the Bible)

"Your word is a lamp to my feet and a light to my path." Psalms 119:105 NASB

Knowing Gods word was critical to me on my way to healing, I had to feed my spirit man just as much as I fed my natural man. Recently, I started reading the bible from front to back. When I start reading it I began seeing myself, my situations, my community, and all the other things that are happening in the world in it. I realized that the things that are happening now are not new, everything that is happening, the Bible prophesied. I would look scriptures up about what I was experiencing and use it to pray or work things out in my mind. I did have to search, research and do some digging, so I could be knowledgeable and completely understand what I was reading. It was very helpful to me.

Knowing Gods word was critical to me on my way to healing. I would look scriptures up about what I was experiencing and use it to pray or work things out in my mind. Recently I started reading the bible from front to back, in reading it I started seeing myself, my situations, my community, and all the other things that are happening in the world in it. I realized that the things that are happening are not new. Everything that is happening now has or has been prophesied from the Bible. I had to feed my spirit man just as much as I feed my natural man. I did have to search, research and do some digging so I could be knowledgeable as I sought to completely understand what I was reading. It was very helpful to me.

The bible has a passage or scripture for everything that we go through in life, children died in the bible as well. We must be able to get our answers through a spiritual context just as much or even more than getting it from a human (doctor or pamphlet). We need to read about what we can do as humans to heal from our wounds. The bible is not just filled with useless verbiage. It helps us to understand why things happen in the world and to us. Believe what is in the Bible, if you don't understand it, get different versions and look things up. We have to be able to go to God in every aspect of our lives, He is so great that He sets it up so that we don't have to want for anything. The Bible is just one of the many things that He gives us freely, use it to get your answers. If you don't know where to start, start from the beginning and work your way to the end. As Pastor Darren would say "Read your bible".

Do you read the Bible? Do you not only read, but do you study for deeper understanding? Do you believe there are things that happen now that is not addressed in the Bible? Do you believe everything in the Bible is true?

All this from that

Delight yourself in the LORD; And He will give you the desired of your heart. Psalms 37:4 NASB

At this point I am doing great; I truly didn't think that I would be at this place in my life.   I have a beautiful family who loves each other, amazing nieces and nephews who I adore and an amazing church family in Columbus, Ohio **Rebirth Worship Center**. I am educated and doing well for myself. However, if someone would have told me, I would be writing a book I would have rolled on the floor from laughter, but I am. I know that Jayla would be so proud of her mommy. I am at a place in my life where not even the sky is the limit for me. I am a walking and living testimony of God's never-failing grace, mercy, and limitless love. I want you to know there is light at the end of the tunnel and like me, you will make it. I encourage you to stick with it and continue to call on the Lord. Please don't give up on God. He is going to make you great if you stick with Him: Psalm 30:5 says "*For His anger is but for a moment, His favor is for a lifetime; Weeping may last for the night, but a shout of joy comes in the morning.*" Your morning is here because you are still standing. If I can make it, so can you. I bless God for you. Do you know how much strength you actually have? You are so strong, God knew that when He created you. Don't give up the fight because you will win. I love you, but God loves you more. Remember where you are going and go win. God Bless You!!!!!

What does your future hold? What do you have planned for the next act of your life? Does your past define you? Does your history

write your future? Are you in control of your future? Do you trust God's plan for your future?

Epilogue

As you read through the sections of the book, were you able to identify the "Five Stages of Grief" that Katrina was experiencing at every turn. This framework identifies the natural cycle many people experience after a loss and brings to light the emotional process experienced as we learn to live after a loss. The stages are tools to help us frame and identify our feelings, but are not stops on some linear timeline in the grieving process.

Within her story Katrina was also able to understand that even though she carried Jayla and her pain was so overwhelming, others were hurting too.

The information about the Grief Cycle was included not to diagnose any type of mental state, but instead as a tool to identify the emotions that may be presented, in an effort to help identify and effectively communicate those emotions to others. The hope is that through utilizing relationships with God and others in your life (that may be experiencing grief as well), those people who care about you and want to support you during this time, to help you through the rough patches. Whether you have someone close to you or not that you are able to share and talk through your feelings, seeking the assistance of a professional and/or support group can be very effective. Sometime hearing supporting and encouraging advice, and other positive reassurances from neutral 3rd party can sometimes be received easier, than from someone close to you, based on history, perception, past interaction and/or bias.

Ultimately, the hope is that you takeaway an understanding that we will go through changes and loss is often one of those changes. One thing that is guaranteed in our life is change. Changes big or small, good or bad, happy or sad, change is not always easy and can turn our world and emotions upside down. But we don't have to stay there and allow our emotions to dictate our path. However, we can use the relationship modeled in "There's Healing after Hurt" to begin the road to healing. There are many resources available to assist you in dealing with the rollercoaster of emotions that are likely to be experienced, have been experienced and/or will be experienced in your journey to healing.

The healingafterhurt.org website will be in a constant state of evolution, as we attempt keep you informed and provide resources, as we find them, that may be helpful to you on your journey. We are here and want to stay connected to you in every way possible, from: sharing your story, writing a letter to your angel, joining an online support group, sharing information that may be helpful to the Healing After Hurt community and creating an avenue for those that are hurting to connect.

Always know that Christ is there to always comfort and heal your broken heart. Even when things happen that we don't understand, it's never by mistake and is always for something greater to be accomplished. Take Katrina when her tears flowed nonstop and she was doing reckless things to cope, no one could have convinced her that she would ever sit down and write this book and not to mention it being published, for all the world to read her secrets, vulnerabilities and all that she went through, the things that have shaped her into the amazing young woman of God she is today.

This book was birthed from the pain that comes with loss, specifically the loss of a child. The loss of Jayla produced pain from her parents never being able to realize any of the dreams that they and her other family members envisioned for her. Loss can be difficult and the loss of a child at any age can be especially heart breaking.

There are several helpful websites available that have a repository of resources;

www.grief.com

https://psychcentral.com/lib/telephone-hotlines-and-help-lines/

http://bereavementireland.com/guides/grieving-the-death-of-a-child/

https://www.change-management-coach.com/kubler-ross.html

Letter to Jayla Kindell Carter

Dear Jayla,

I am writing you this letter, to let you know how I am doing down here on Earth, while you are up in heaven. Baby girl, I wish with all of my might that I could have held you, fed you, changed you and experienced all of the difficulties that come with motherhood. I am certain that you would have been an excellent daughter. However, God saw fit for you to be with him and while it was not easy at first, I have peace that you are in a place where you will never experience hurt, pain, disappointment, or feelings of low self-worth. You are with our Father and Lord, and that is better than any place I could have given you here.

After losing you, you will be proud to know that I still fought to finish and obtained my associates degree in Early Childhood Education. I am still in the healing phase of losing you and with every day that passes, I am stronger. I am also back in college to receive my bachelor's degree in Early Childhood Education, as well. One of my biggest accomplishments, is I have received the strength to write a book about the things that I dealt with after losing you. This is my way of helping other mothers, fathers, and families to connect with each other, open the lines of communication, and begin to heal. I have you to thank for that and I am so grateful to have given you the nutrients that you needed and felt you inside of my belly for the months that I did. I will never forget about you and when the time comes, I will tell your younger brothers and sisters about you. Until we meet again in Heaven, I love you with my entire heart baby girl.

Love your mother,

Katrina

Share Your Story or A Letter to Your Lost Love One.

The Journey to healing shared in "There is Healing After Hurt" (THaH) is not an isolated incident. Through the writing of this book, the team God sent to bring it to fruition, encountered many moms, dads, sisters, brothers, aunts, uncles and many other family members that they themselves or someone they knew, had experienced the same type of loss. The team found, the common reaction to the subject of this book was, the experience is very difficult for many involved and they wished there had been something like this book to read and/or share with someone they knew might benefit from it.

Do you know someone or are you someone that has gone through a situation similar experience as Katrina? Were you able to navigate the grieve process a bit better than Katrina? Would this resource have been beneficial for your healing journey?

The Call to Action – Share Your Story

We would love to hear your story and maybe in sharing it might bring some healing to someone else going through their journey or help you in your own. As mentioned in the book, the parents aren't alone in experiencing the loss, with that we want to hear your stories. The stories can come from any and everyone's perspective. The hope is the compilation of stories can touch and comfort each reader in a relatable way.

Would you be interested in sharing your story? Would you be interested in seeing it shared in print? Where would you start your story?

Write a letter to you lost little love.

We would love to have you share a letter to your lost little love. What would you like to say to your little one? What would you like to share with your little one about you now and what has changed since you lost them? Share your hopes and dreams, their siblings, opportunities you took advantage of (school, career, travel, support of others experiencing lost) … Writing letters is often a great tool to aid in the healing process and often provides much needed closure that allows people to get unstuck. The letter does not have to be to a premature baby; rather it can be to any child that died before reaching their full life.

Would you like to write a letter to your angel? Would you be interested in sharing it with others and see it in print with other similar letters? You can begin writing you letter here…

Discussion Group Questions

- Who are you? How would you describe yourself in three words?
- Has there been an event in your life that you felt caught you off guard? The derailed your planned path?
- What day would you say was "That Day"? The day that changed the trajectory of your life?
- Who is your support system? Do they hold you accountable for your actions/ decisions?
- Do you blame yourself for things outside of your control? Do you beat yourself up for things that don't go right in your life?
- What have you done that you are proud of? What do you currently do that you are proud of?
- What things do you have to be intentional about to keep moving forward?
- What goal(s) do you need to evaluate or reevaluate?
- What things do you need to positively change how you speak about them?
- What part of Katrina's story resonated most for you?
- When you read Katrina's story was there any one who you could instantly think of that had a similar experience and could be help by reading her story?
- Will you share this book with someone else? If you have taken notes in your book will you recommend it to others?
- What is the best way you could describe "THaH"?
- Did you find that you were able to get something out of the book even if you have never lost a child?